D1475849

The SPORTS HEROES Library

WINNERS NEVER QUIT
Athletes Who Beat the Odds

Nathan Aaseng

Lerner Publications Company • Minneapolis

To Bill and Dorothy

LIBRARY OF CONGRESS CATALOGING IN PUBLICATION DATA

Aaseng, Nathan.
Winners never quit.

(The Sports heroes library)
SUMMARY: Brief biographies of 10 athletes who achieved
greatness while overcoming a handicap or misfortune. Includes
Bobby Clarke, Wes Unseld, Rocky Bleier, John Hiller, Kitty
O'Neil, Lee Trevino, Tom Dempsey, Larry Brown, Ron LeFlore,
and Tommy John.

1. Athletes—Biography—Juvenile literature. 2. Handicapped
—Biography—Juvenile literature. [1. Athletes. 2. Physically
handicapped] I. Title.

GV697.A1A23   1980   796'.092'2 [B] [920]   80-12305
ISBN 0-8225-1060-X   (lib. bdg.)

Manufactured in the United States of America

International Standard Book Number: 0-8225-1060-X
Library of Congress Catalog Card Number: 80-12305

2 3 4 5 6 7 8 9 10 90 89 88 87 86 85 84 83 82 81

Contents

Tom Dempsey holds the record for the longest field goal ever kicked —63 yards.

Introduction

This book is about sports heroes who probably should *not* have been stars. Usually only an athlete with extraordinary talent, a healthy body, and good luck reaches the top of the sports world. None of the 10 athletes you will read about in this book has been blessed with all three.

Football's Rocky Bleier and basketball's Wes Unseld had only average skills even before their legs were seriously damaged. Larry Brown battled bad luck, pain, and deafness on his way to a pro football career. Kitty O'Neil's deafness did not keep her from setting an incredible string of athletic records. Lee Trevino struggled with the misfortune of being a poor boy trying to play an expensive sport, golf. Both John Hiller and Tommy John pitched their best seasons *after* their careers seemed shattered by health problems. Bobby

Through patience and hard work, Tommy John was able to overcome pain and disability and resume his pitching career.

Clarke's courage in fighting diabetes stayed with him on the hockey rink. Tom Dempsey managed to set pro football kicking records with less than half a foot. And Ron LeFlore started his baseball career behind the walls of a prison.

Most people who lack talent, good health, or luck only have wild dreams about becoming stars. But these 10 athletes set out after the goal of becoming sports heroes. They refused to give up until they had become winners.

These "extra effort" heroes are some of the most admired people in sports. Why? When the world's super athletes perform, everyone marvels at their skill. Many must shrug and wish they had been as talented and lucky to have such skill. But when the extra effort heroes battle to the top, players and fans may still marvel at their performance, but they no longer envy these stars. For they realize that they might be winners, too, if they work hard enough.

The athletes in this book bring something special to sports. Everyone loves to see underdogs do well. No one would be excited to watch a person push open the lid of a box and climb out. But if a hand-cuffed person were placed in a box with huge locks on it, lowered into a tub of water, and then tried to climb out, that would be thrilling to see. The extra effort heroes, like the person in the locked box, seem to face hopeless problems. Yet they work and work until they find a way to overcome their problems. They make the most of their abilities.

There's a familiar saying, "It's not whether you win or lose, but how you play the game." The 10 athletes in this book are all winners. But the real key to their success is how they played the game.

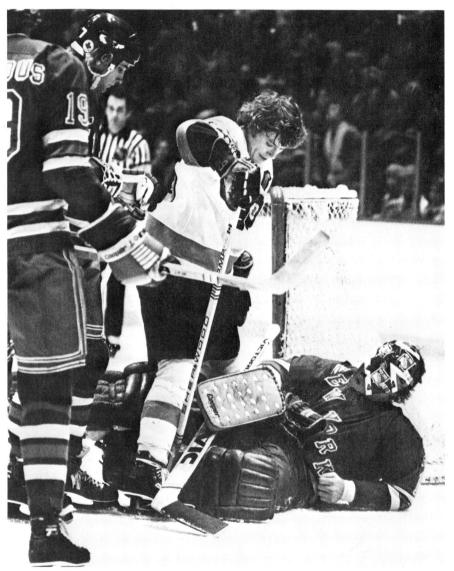

Diabetes has not slowed down Bobby Clarke of the Philadelphia Flyers. He is one of the top players in the National Hockey League.

8

1
Bobby Clarke

The stadium was packed for the 1974 Stanley Cup finals of the National Hockey League. The Philadelphia Flyers lined up against the Boston Bruins for the face-off. Bobby Clarke and his Boston opponent waited in the face-off circle. When the referee dropped the puck, the two men lunged at it with their sticks. As usual, Bobby Clarke gained control of the puck.

In that championship series, Bobby won three of every four face-offs. Few people keep track of who wins face-offs, but Bobby's skill at it helped the Flyers win the series. Controlling face-offs is only one example of what Bobby does to help his team win hockey games. No one in hockey works harder and finds so many ways to win.

Bobby Clarke plays center for Philadelphia. When his team must skate shorthanded because of a penalty, he is usually on the ice to help until the penalty is over. When the other team is short a player, he is on the ice again to lead the attack.

Bobby has always played hard on the ice, even as a boy. Perhaps it was one way of keeping warm in his hometown of Flin Flon, Manitoba. Flin Flon is a mining town that lies in northern Canada. Boys who grew up in Flin Flon often went to work in the mines. Bobby didn't want to take up mining. He wanted to play professional hockey.

Bobby hardly looked like the ideal hockey idol. He was small, wore dark-rimmed glasses, and had buck teeth. Then, when Bobby was 14, his family discovered that he had a disease called diabetes. In order to keep the disease under control, he had to give himself shots every day. Bobby was told that the only way he could continue to play hockey was as a goalie because he wouldn't have to skate so much. But Bobby did not want to be a goalie. He went out and proved that he could still skate hard. He did so well that in 1969 he was considered the best junior player in western Canada. The National Hockey League, however, paid more attention to

In 1980 Bobby was named the Most Courageous Athlete of the Decade by the Philadelphia Sports Writers Association.

medical reports than to Bobby's hockey record. Several teams passed up the chance to get Clarke that year. Only Philadelphia decided he was worth a try.

Even though he did not know where Philadelphia was, Bobby was excited. When he reported for his first practice, he was a little *too* excited, and he fainted on the ice! The Flyers must have thought he really did belong in bed. But Bobby had merely forgotten to eat breakfast that morning. After that, the Flyers made sure he followed regular eating patterns to keep his diabetes under control.

With that scare out of the way, Bobby showed what he could do on the ice. In practices and games, he raced around like a fireball on ice. He could make perfect passes to teammates and fire shots like all good hockey players. But he could also poke, shove, crawl, and scramble after the puck. Bobby tried everything to disturb his opponents— from chattering at them to banging into them.

After a while, opponents began looking out for him. It was a terrible feeling not knowing where Bobby was, or what he was up to. They just knew he was ready to try something. Clarke's style of play made him an instant favorite in Philadelphia. When teammates saw Bobby working so hard, it made them try all the harder.

At the age of 23, Bobby was named team captain, even though he was one of the Flyers' youngest

Bobby always has his eyes on the action, even when he's not in the middle of it.

players. He was perfect for the role. He was good at encouraging his teammates to try harder. One time Bobby talked to a player who was in a slump, and that teammate came back to score three goals the next night. Even when there was only a slim chance of winning, Bobby would insist that the best line play more. Yet he was always concerned that others had a chance to skate.

Bobby's great speed and agility enable him to skate around larger defenders.

In 1975 the Flyers took a quick, two-game lead in the play-off series. Everyone was thrilled, and the team owner even began throwing parties as if the series were over. The overconfident Flyers began losing. Bobby angrily told the owner and the players that the time for celebrating was *after* the series, not before. The Flyers responded by winning the remaining games.

Besides being a natural leader, Bobby is an excellent hockey player. He comes up with the big plays. In the 1974 Stanley Cup Championship series, Bobby won one game with a goal in overtime. He also set up important goals in the other games and helped Philadelphia win the title. Bobby repeated his performance the next year, and Philadelphia again won the Stanley Cup. Three times Bobby has been named the League's Most Valuable Player.

Bobby's leadership qualities were recognized again when the Flyers' management made him assistant coach for the 1979-80 season. As assistant coach, Bobby had even more responsibility for the team's play than when he had been captain. And that suited him just fine.

Throughout his playing career, Bobby's coach had only one complaint about his star player. And that was that Bobby was *too* unselfish. Bobby could shoot more than he did, but instead he spent too much time looking to see if someone was in a better position to score. He always liked to make sure the person in the best position took the shot.

The folks back in Flin Flon know all about Bobby's unselfishness, too. Once they wanted to give a huge dinner in his honor, but he would not allow it. Bobby said that *he* should be the one thanking *them* for their encouragement and support over the years.

All through his playing years, Bobby Clarke was always easy to spot on the hockey rink. He was the player who had so much energy—the guy who was supposed to be too sick to skate!

2
Wes
Unseld

Among all the long-legged leapers of professional basketball, Wes Unseld seemed out of place. He was shorter than all other pro centers. Because of bad knees, he could barely jump and did not run fast. Washington Bullet fans had trouble remembering the last time they saw him dribble the ball. Wes did not thrill crowds by dunking. In fact, he hardly ever scored. Besides all that, his free-throw shooting was so poor that opponents sometimes fouled him on purpose.

It sounded like Wes would not last two seconds in the pros. Yet in 1980, he finished his 12th season as starter on one of basketball's best teams, the Bullets. In spite of all his disadvantages, Wes, who retired after the 1980-81 season, was considered one of the National Basketball

Association's best players. What's the reason? Wes knew how to use his two main skills: brains and strength. He also knew how to be in the right spot at the right time. Once 250-pound Unseld planted his feet, nothing but a tornado could uproot him.

Wesley Unseld grew up in Louisville, Kentucky. In high school, he used his muscular body to overpower foes in basketball. Some big colleges that had only allowed white players on their teams decided that Wes was too strong a player to pass up. Wes knew that his rugged style of play and stubborn manner would be a handicap if he were in the spotlight as "the first black basketball player." So he stayed at home and went to Louisville University.

At Louisville Wes was the nation's leading rebounder his junior year. In 1967 and 1968, he was named to All-American teams. Though his strengths were defense and rebounding, he managed to score 23 points per game in his final year.

At 6 feet, 7 inches, Wes was considered too short to play center for the pros. But the Bullets (then playing in Baltimore) decided to recruit him, and Wes wasted no time proving himself. He joined the team in 1968, and the Bullets became winners. Wes pulled down over 18 rebounds a game his first year.

Wes Unseld could fly high, even though his knees were operated on three times.

19

Not only did he win Rookie of the Year honors, he was also named the League's Most Valuable Player! Wilt Chamberlain was the only other player to earn both titles his first year in the pros.

Teammates knew that playing with Wes made the game more fun. He had a way of making his fellow Bullets look even better than they already were. When Wes charged after a rebound, his teammates raced for the other basket. Wes usually wrestled the ball away from opponents. Then he whirled around and zipped an overhand pass to a teammate halfway down the court. Often the teammate would outrun the other team's defense and make an easy basket. On offense Wes let his teammates take the shots while he set up "screens" for them. Bullet players dribbled as near to Wes as they could. The man guarding them then ran into Wes. This left the Bullets free to take an unhurried shot. It was hard enough for opponents to guard one man without having to chase around Wes.

While Wes helped make his team look good on offense, one of his defensive jobs was to make the other team look bad. He did not soar high to block shots. But his hefty body clogged up the lanes around the basket. Foes could not muscle through

Wes Unseld

or find room to move. After nights of bumps and bruises against Wes, some centers felt like they had been in a football game. Wes was able to keep opponents from going where they wanted without fouling them. He had quick hands for a large man and stole many passes.

Despite all of these successes, Wes played most of his career in pain. His knees were operated on three times. Because of his operations, he could not run or jump the way he once could.

In spite of his many injuries, Wes was one of the strongest players in the National Basketball Association.

Before one game, he had enough water drained from one knee to fill a large glass! In 1973 he couldn't practice and played in only 56 games. Wes seemed ready to retire.

Yet Wes missed few games since then. He wore a scowl most of the time when he played. Because of the pain in his knees, basketball was mostly hard work for him. But he did his job.

The scowl sometimes made him look like an unfriendly person. But off the court he was pleasant and interesting to talk with. He loved to read books. He has been honored many times for his volunteer work in Washington, D.C. During the off-season, he helped with a summer basketball league for kids.

In 1978 Wes came up with the most important plays of his career. In the second round of the National Basketball Association (NBA) play-offs, he made a basket from a rebound to beat the favored Philadelphia 76ers. When Washington reached the championship series against Seattle, Wes had a good reason for wanting to win. He had played in two other championships, and both times his team had lost four games in a row. This time Washington and Seattle each won three games. Washington was ahead in the second half of the last game. In the final minutes, the Bullets had only a two-point lead. Seattle's best chance of winning was to foul quickly and hope the Bullets missed the free throw. This would stop the clock and give Seattle a last chance to send the game into overtime.

The Bullets' coach knew what Seattle wanted to do. He tried to get Wes out of the game since the burly guy was not a good free-throw shooter. But Wes was fouled before that could happen. With the outcome of the game and the championship in his hands, Wes made both shots. The Bullets were finally champions!

As usual, Wes had not scored much in the series. He did not make graceful moves or spectacular shots. Seattle did not have to worry about his blocking shots. For most NBA centers, this would have made it a disappointing series. But when the officials checked out all the important but unnoticed parts of the game, they had to admit Wes had done his job. It was Wes who helped make his teammates look good and the opponents look bad. Even Wes allowed himself a small smile when he was given the trophy for Most Valuable Player in the series.

3
Rocky
Bleier

Rocky Bleier was in bad shape when he returned home from Viet Nam in 1969. His legs had been hit by both a bullet and a grenade. He limped and could not use several toes on his right foot. According to the army, Rocky could perform just over half of what a normal army man could.

Even so, Rocky still wanted to play football. This hard-hitting sport is dangerous enough for large, healthy men. How long could a small, 5-foot, 10-inch wounded war veteran last? It would have been almost impossible to make up for his injuries, even if Rocky had fantastic skill. But Rocky had been lucky enough just to make the Pittsburgh Steelers' team before he went to Viet Nam. The Steelers had been one of the worst teams in football at that time. Somehow Rocky battled his way back to a starting job with the team. Not only that, but he played an important role in Pittsburgh's four Super Bowl championships.

Rocky grew up in Appleton, Wisconsin. He went to a private school that won nearly every football and basketball game they played. For college, he chose Notre Dame, another private school with a strong sports program. There he played in the national college football championship his junior year. Pro scouts crowded around Notre Dame's practice fields to look at the school's fine players. But Rocky was barely noticed. The scouts who did look at him were not impressed. He was not big, fast, or very much of a hitter, and his running moves didn't fool anyone.

The Pittsburgh Steelers finally drafted him in 1968, only after 416 other players had been chosen. Fortunately, Pittsburgh's other runners were not much better. Rocky earned himself a seat on the bench for his rookie season.

Late that season, he found his career in trouble. Someone else had drafted him—the United States Army. Rocky was sent over to Viet Nam to fight.

Rocky Bleier's career with the Pittsburgh Steelers was interrupted by the Viet Nam War. He received leg and foot injuries that nearly ended his football career.

In 1969 the North Vietnamese ambushed Rocky's patrol. Rocky felt a bullet slam into one leg. While he was lying there, a grenade sent metal bits into his other leg. Luckily, another soldier hauled him to safety.

Badly wounded, Rocky was sent home. The doctors told him to forget about playing football again. But Rocky had to give it a try. When he worked out for the first time, he learned how tough it was going to be. Instead of running, all he could manage was a flat-footed limp. He collapsed after a short run, out of breath.

Rocky refused to give up and followed a rigorous training schedule. He was up at dawn to run several miles. Then he would lift weights for a couple of hours, do sprints for an hour, and finish by running up and down steps. From the way he looked in the early part of training camp, even his teammates thought he was wasting his time. He still looked awkward and flat-footed. Since everyone liked Rocky, they didn't want to see him get hurt. Even the coach wanted him to find another job. In the end, Rocky was cut from the team. But the Steelers' owner, Art Rooney, told him to have his foot operated on and try again.

Rocky has proven the importance of dedication in overcoming a handicap.

Rocky did just that. The Steelers still had only a few good runners, and Rocky showed just enough courage to make the team again. Through the 1970 and 1971 seasons, Rocky never carried the ball. Even he had to admit he was getting nowhere. Before the 1972 season, he decided it would be his last. But once again, Mr. Rooney came through for him. He told Rocky that the Steelers were pleased with his efforts. Rocky was finally encouraged to stay with football.

With this encouragement, Rocky stepped up his workouts during the winter. By the 1973 season, his teammates hardly recognized him. He had built himself up from 185 to 216 pounds and was one of the strongest men on the team. Some of his friends called him Boulder instead of Rocky! The effect of his sprint work was even more amazing. He no longer ran like a large duck. In fact, he could beat all but a few Steelers in a sprint.

Still Rocky had been such an ordinary player for so long that the coaches paid little attention to him. His only chance to play was with the special squads that take the field for kickoffs and punts. Rocky figured that he would just have to impress the coaches on these teams. He charged fearlessly into walls of huge blockers. He blasted into everyone in sight who wore a different uniform.

In 1974 the coaches finally had to admit that this wounded veteran could play some tough football. It did not matter so much that he was not a fancy runner. Pittsburgh already had star Franco Harris, a speedy 230-pounder, to carry the ball. With Rocky in the backfield, it would be just like having an extra lineman to block for Franco. Rocky paved the way as Harris piled up large chunks of yardage.

In 1980 Rocky played in his fourth Super Bowl game for the Steelers.

When Rocky showed he could run the ball as well as block, it was an extra bonus. He was a straight-ahead runner who never danced around looking for openings. As a result, he rarely broke through for long runs or looked very flashy. He doesn't even like to watch himself on films. But his style of running is beautiful to his linemen. They know that if they hold their block for a split second, Rocky won't hesitate. And they don't have to guess where he is going to run. They know he's heading straight downfield.

In 1975 the Steelers won their first Super Bowl in Rocky's first year as a starter. The following year, Rocky proved that he was more than an extra lineman to block for Harris. He gained over 1,000 yards to rank as one of the season's best rushers in football. Again he helped the Steelers to a Super Bowl win. In the 1979 Super Bowl against Dallas, Rocky played an important part in Pittsburgh's third championship. He grabbed a touchdown pass with one hand while falling backward. His stunning catch gave the Steelers just enough of a lead to hold off the Cowboys, 34-31.

Rocky retired after the 1980 season, completing 11 years in the NFL. That was not a bad record for a man the U.S. Army said was 40 percent disabled. And anyone who had met him head-on in a football game wouldn't have believed it!

4
John
Hiller

Until 1971 John Hiller spent most of his time as a professional pitcher watching from behind the fence in the left field bullpen. He did have a few good games with the Detroit Tigers. In his first two starts, he did not allow a single run. But there were enough bad performances so that his team did not risk letting him pitch in important situations.

John found little to do in the bullpen, so he just sat around. His weight ballooned to 220 pounds, and he did not watch his health. In the winter of 1971, Hiller barely survived a heart attack. He says it was the best thing that ever happened to him! Very few people feel lucky to have a heart attack. These attacks are dangerous and kill many people every year.

At first John did not feel lucky. Doctors said he would need a serious operation to stay alive. His baseball career seemed over. But the heart attack made John stop and see what he had been doing with his life. He did not like what he saw. Heart attacks usually happen to older people, and John was only 25. But he ate, drank, and smoked so much that his body was wearing down. John also discovered that he had not been exercising enough. For a man who played sports for a living, this was almost unbelievable! All these things had caused the heart attack.

While the rest of his teammates began the 1971 season, John started watching his health. He practiced pitching by throwing a ball at a cement block in his backyard. He hoped he would someday get another chance to prove himself. While he practiced, his money started to run out. The Hillers had to give up their home and cut back on expenses.

When John showed up at the 1972 Tigers' training camp, some Detroit officials worried. Major league baseball is no place for a man with a weak heart, they figured. So John was given an easier job as minor league pitching coach. This was not what John wanted, but he hoped he would get a chance before long.

John Hiller of the Detroit Tigers played his best baseball after recovering from a near-fatal heart attack.

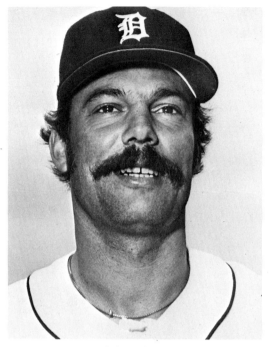
John Hiller

The chance came in July. Detroit's left-handed
pitchers were being clobbered. They needed a good
lefty like Hiller. Doctors finally convinced the team
that Hiller could pitch in tense situations with no
danger. When John returned to the old left field
bullpen weighing 40 pounds less, he looked like a
new man. He did not get rattled when he entered
a close game with men on base. Compared to his
narrow escape from death, the most tense moment

on the field seemed like a peaceful stroll on the beach. Coolly, he stopped rally after rally.

Even if he still wanted to sit around in the bull-pen, the Tigers did not give him the chance. In 1973, his first full season after recovery, he pitched in more games than anyone else in the league and was named Comeback Player of the Year. In the next six years, John became one of the finest relief pitchers in baseball history. His fastball seemed to change course just when it reached the plate. Many Detroit games ended with an opponent's swinging at and missing a Hiller pitch. For some batters, just getting a base hit off John was an achievement.

John's best seasons were 1973 and 1974. In 1973 he had 38 saves, a league record. (A save is awarded when a relief pitcher keeps his team in the lead to the end of the game.) That year he gave up less than one run for every six innings he pitched. In 1974 he won 17 games, setting an American League record for wins by a relief pitcher. Starting pitchers usually get credit for most of the wins, but Hiller's 17 victories topped most of the starters in the league.

Though his comeback was successful, John faced other problems in his career. In 1975 he had struck out 87 men in just 71 innings before an injury finished his season early. In 1977 a liver ailment was partly to blame for his only poor year of pitching. Just as before, he regained his health and pitched well in 1978.

The Detroit Tigers liked John for reasons other than his good pitching. Ever since the Tigers scouted him on a sandlot in Toronto, Hiller had played for no one but Detroit. And he remained there until his retirement in 1980. While many players became free agents and signed for millions of dollars with the team that made the best offer, John's main interest wasn't money. His friends and the ball club that had given him a second chance were worth more to him.

At one time John was a brash, slightly conceited young man. But after his heart attack, he seemed much calmer to his friends and did not seek glory. He wanted to inspire other heart attack victims to fight back from their illnesses. Few people get a second chance at life, not to mention a career as a professional baseball player. So John wanted to make sure he did things right the second time around.

5
Kitty
O'Neil

It was only fitting that Kitty O'Neil should appear in the television series "The Bionic Woman." Kitty may come the closest of any woman to accomplishing what the bionic woman can do. It seems that whenever Kitty has a spare minute, she finds a new sport and beats everyone at it. She has been an Olympic diver, a Hollywood stuntwoman, and a world record holder in two other sports.

Kitty, however, has not been blessed with extraordinary powers. In fact, she doesn't even have all the powers that most people have. She has been totally deaf since she was baby. She stands barely 5 feet, 3 inches tall and weighs about 100 pounds. But none of this has stopped her from doing amazing feats.

On December 6, 1976, Kitty O'Neil reached 618 miles per hour to set a new women's land speed record. Her goal is to break the sound barrier.

Kitty was born in Corpus Christi, Texas. Before she was one year old, she had suffered from measles, mumps, and small pox. Kitty survived all three, but her hearing did not.

When Kitty's father was killed in a plane crash, her mother was left to raise her. Mrs. O'Neil, a full-blooded Cherokee Indian, went to school to learn how to teach the deaf to communicate. With her mother's help, Kitty quickly learned to read lips and speak. Though she has never been able to hear what her words sound like, her speech is nearly normal. Kitty's mother also taught her to swim.

By third grade, Kitty was ready for regular school. There she showed how well she could get along in a silent world. She learned to play the cello and the piano by sensing the vibrations made by the instruments!

Kitty also went out for the school swim team, and it was one of the few times she did not excel at a sport. But when Kitty filled in for the swim team diver, one day, she was awarded first place! She had never finished that high in her regular events.

Kitty became such a skilled diver that she moved to Anaheim, California, at the age of 16 to train under Dr. Sammy Lee, a former Olympic champion. Dr. Lee liked to shout instructions to divers while they were in the air. Of course, Kitty could not hear them, so Dr. Lee fired blanks in a gun to send signals to her. Kitty could feel the shock made by the explosions.

She learned a lot from Dr. Lee and moved quickly to the top in diving competition. Though bothered by a broken wrist in training, she finished eighth in the 1964 Tokyo Olympics. Kitty seemed ready to do even better, but she came down with a serious illness—spinal meningitis. Some people thought she would never walk again.

Kitty recovered, but her diving days were over. Rather than feel bad about it, Kitty looked for other sports she could try. She found that racing, running, scuba diving, skydiving, and waterskiing were all exciting, too. Kitty worked hard and in 1970 she set a women's speed record for waterskiing, zooming over the water at more than 104 miles per hour.

In 1976 Kitty married a stuntman. A stuntperson performs dangerous tricks for TV and movies so that the stars do not hurt themselves. These tricks looked like fun to Kitty. It was hardly a safe way to make a living, but Kitty, as usual, was fearless.

Kitty was the first stuntwoman to perform the dangerous fully engulfed firegag. For this stunt, she wore nearly 100 pounds of equipment, including a four-layer asbestos suit and a 50-pound helmet.

"Being deaf is not a handicap," says Kitty. "It is a challenge to conquer, similar to being called on to do a difficult stunt."

It took her just a few months to become an expert, and soon she was performing stunts in *Omen II, Airport 77*, and other movies. She also stunted for such television series as "Quincy," "The Bionic Woman," "Police Woman," "Wonder Woman," and "Baretta."

Kitty has done stunts involving fire, water, cars, motorcycles, boats, riding horseback, high falls, and fight scenes. Some of her stunts, such as her high falls into water (from over 100 feet) and her fall onto an airbag (from 127 feet for Wonder Woman), have not yet been attempted by other women. Kitty is also the only woman who has done the fully engulfed fire gag.

Kitty is an expert in most sports, including karate, and is the only female member of an elite motion picture professional stunt organization. Kitty is able to concentrate so well that her mind seems to work like a computer. Rather than learn from her mistakes, she seems to have the mistakes ironed out *before* she makes her first attempts.

To most people, this would seem like enough excitement for one lifetime. But in 1976, Kitty decided that the women's land speed record needed breaking. At Dry Lake, Oregon, in a three-wheeled land missile, she broke the old record with an average speed of 308 miles per hour. That was not enough for her. The next time out, she set another record time of 512 miles per hour (average speed) while rocketing to a top speed of 618 miles per hour. She reached such a speed that it took her five miles to come to a stop! Kitty's next goal is to break the sound barrier and the current land speed record of 739 miles per hour.

One reason Kitty does not seem to fear anything is that she is a very religious woman. She also believes that being deaf should not stop her from doing what anyone else can. Not only can Kitty do what others can, but she almost always does it better.

6
Lee
Trevino

Peering through fences, young Lee Trevino watched the golfers enviously. He saw them practicing their shots and taking golf lessons on the freshly cut course. Though he lived right next to a golf course, he might as well have been 1,000 miles away. He had no money to play.

Lee was born of Mexican parents in 1939. His father ran away one day, leaving Lee with his mother and his grandfather, who was a poor gravedigger. They lived in a shack in a hayfield near Dallas, Texas. Lee had no friends, so he spent his time hanging around the nearby golf course. One day he found a five-iron club that someone had forgotten or thrown away. Lee practiced using it on anything that happened to be small and round. He finally got onto the golf course by taking a job there. After work he could practice.

During the 1979 season, Lee Trevino became the second player to reach two million dollars in official winnings. Jack Nicklaus was the first.

Lee's life changed in the next few years. He quit school in the eighth grade to earn money for his family. Later he joined the marines. When he returned to Dallas in 1960, he had only one goal: to play golf.

In pursuing his goal, Lee never seemed to run out of energy. He would wake up early in the morning to play golf. From there he would work at a job all day. Then he would stay out most of the night and be ready to start all over again at dawn.

Months of whacking 1,000 golf balls a day paid off for Lee. In 1963 and 1965, he won the Texas State Open for amateurs. Finally, he felt ready to take on the pros. But the professional golf organization in Dallas would not accept him as a member. Lee felt he was being discriminated against and went to New Mexico where he was accepted as a pro.

Being a pro does not mean instant riches, however. Pros must earn a lot of money just to pay their expenses. Lee only made $600 his first year on the tour. Just when he was most desperate for money, he placed sixth in the 1967 U.S. Open and earned $6,000. That tournament became the launching pad for Lee's career. The following year, 1968, he won the Open and moved into the top ranks of golf.

1981 marked the 14th consecutive season in which Lee Trevino won at least one major tournament.

Besides his unusual beginnings, Lee drew attention as a colorful sports figure. While most of his fellow pros were serious and business-like on the course, Lee was full of chatter and jokes. Once Lee was about to tee off against Jack Nicklaus in a very important match. At such a serious time, Lee pulled a rubber snake out of his bag and tossed it at Nicklaus. Nicklaus laughed, but the officials did not think it was so funny.

Golf experts do not know what to think of Trevino. Since he has not received the best training, he has what many consider a technically poor swing. At a stocky 5 feet, 7 inches, he is somewhat oddly built for a golfer. Yet few can match Lee's well-placed drives off the tee. Lee has also built himself up from an average putter to a very good one.

"Poor" swing and all, Lee became the hottest golfer on the pro tour. In 50 tournaments from 1968 to 1971, he finished in the top 10. Amazingly, Lee snatched the U.S., Canadian, and British opens all in one summer—1971. For his efforts, he was named Sportsman of the Year by *Sports Illustrated* magazine. Lee was especially proud of having the lowest average score of the pros two years in a row.

Before long, he was known as Super Mex. Crowds of fans who called themselves Lee's Fleas tagged along whenever he played. Lee continued winning until 1975 when two misfortunes struck him. First, he was hit by lightning during a golf round. The burns he received were only minor, but it was a scary experience. Later, Lee developed a back problem that nearly finished his golfing career. But Lee quietly battled back after an operation. Though he did not win as often, he moved up in the standings until he was again one of the top money-winners on the tour. When Lee again won the Canadian Open in 1979 and the Tournament of Champions in 1981, he ranked as one of the all-time high money winners in golf. In 1981 Trevino was also elected to the World Golf Hall of Fame.

Lee gives some of his earnings to charity and uses his excellent speaking ability for a variety of worthwhile causes. He has made many friends because he makes a point of attending some of the smaller tournaments that other pros usually skip. Lee's good public image starts on the golf course. Once a TV crew planned to interview Lee before a round. They were caught in traffic and arrived when Lee was ready to tee off. The crew thought they had blown their chance, but Lee signaled them to set up their cameras. After he hit his drive, he walked over to talk to the crew. Then he raced ahead to his companions so they would not have to wait for him. Instead of nothing, the TV crew wound up with an excellent story. Lee managed to find a way to work things out, just as he has done for most of his career in golf.

7

Tom Dempsey

Tom Dempsey put up with a lot of teasing as a youngster. One look at him and you could see his body was different. His shriveled right arm had no hand on it, and he had less than half of a right foot. Tom was born that way in 1947 in Milwaukee, Wisconsin. His family moved to California two years later. During the next 10 years, Tom had 16 operations on his arm and foot. Though other kids made him feel handicapped, Tom's dad convinced him to ignore their attitude. His dad told him he could do anything that a "normal" person could do. To prove it, he played all kinds of sports with Tom.

In 1978 Tom kicked 36 extra points for the Buffalo Bills and missed only 2.

When Tom entered high school, he learned that his father had been right. He played football and wrestled. On the junior college level, he met stiffer challenges but continued to do well. At Palomor Junior College in California, he made all-conference football teams as a defensive end. He continued to wrestle and even put the shot for the college track team.

While at college, Tom tried place-kicking a football. He found that his stubby foot could work to his advantage. Because his foot was so small and light, he could swing it faster than the other kickers. He also did not have to worry about holding his foot steady—it was locked stiff whether he liked it or not. Of course, his foot was not tailor-made for kicking. His short foot, like a short barrel on a gun, was less accurate than a long foot.

In 1969 Tom joined the New Orleans Saints. The poor Saints had given their fans little to cheer about through the years, but Tom was one bright spot. Wearing a special wedge-shaped shoe, Tom made 61 percent of his field goal tries that year. His 22 field goals and 33 extra point kicks added up to 99 points, making him one of the top scorers in the league. This was amazing considering how few

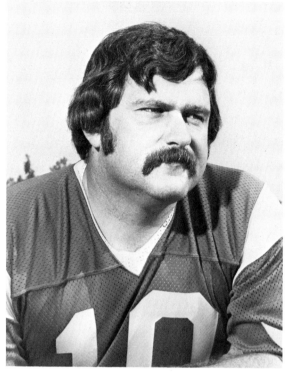

Tom Dempsey

times the Saints moved into scoring position. The
big, 263-pound rookie impressed so many people
that he made the National Football League's All-
Star team!

In 1970 Tom kicked a record-breaking field goal.
The Saints were playing the Detroit Lions in a
close, tough game. Tom's three field goals had
helped, but Detroit still held a 17 to 16 lead. With
seconds to go, New Orleans had time for just one
attempt at scoring. Their only chance seemed to

be a desperate long pass. The Lions could hardly believe it then, when the Saints' field goal team came out on the field. The ball sat 55 yards from the goal posts! Tom would have to add at least 7 yards onto that to be safe from any blockers. In fact, Tom had his holder crouch 8 yards back to make sure he had time to kick.

The snap from the center was good, and the astonished Lions didn't put a hard rush on the kicker. Tom took a few quick strides and swung his foot into the ball. The ball sailed up toward the goal posts, which looked tiny in the distance. Tom could not even see if the ball was going through them. But the crowd's roar and the sight of Lions' burying their faces in their hands told him. His 63-yard field goal attempt was good! Tom not only set a distance record, but the Saints won the game 19 to 17.

Nevertheless, Tom did not kick for the Saints much longer. Though he was no heavier than the year before, coaches gave him trouble about his weight in preseason practice. Bothered by criticism, Tom began spraying the ball to all sides of the field. Less than a year after his 63-yard field goal, Tom was dropped from the team.

Tom played for the Philadelphia Eagles from 1971 to 1974.

The Philadelphia Eagles remembered how well Tom had once kicked and in 1971 signed him to the team. He led the league in field goal accuracy that year. His long-range missiles seemed to have a homing device that guided the ball through the posts. He broke the Eagles' record for longest kick that year.

Then in 1975 Tom went to the Los Angeles Rams. That year he proved that he still had some good kicks left in him. He made an excellent 21 of 26 field goal tries. He has since played just as well for the Houston Oilers and the Buffalo Bills.

Tom has been admired for his efforts both on and off the field. A Philadelphia organization named him Man of the Year in 1971, both for his athletic ability and for visiting handicapped persons in hospitals. Tom insists that he is not really handicapped and does not want special attention because of his foot and arm. In fact, he wears regular-looking shoes off the field. Tom says that everyone has some kind of handicap. He just happens to have one that people notice.

After struggling on losing teams most of his life, Larry Brown finally found a home with the winning Washington Redskins in 1969.

8
Larry Brown

Like most of the people in the ghettos of Pittsburgh, the Brown family struggled to make a living. Larry Brown rarely saw his father, who worked two jobs to support them. Unlike some of his friends who ended up in jail, were killed, or got into drugs, Larry survived childhood.

Larry's chance to escape this life was through sports. Though he was deaf in one ear, and played for a losing high school team, he showed enough ability to attract a few college football offers. By the time he made up his mind to go to college, one offer remained—Dodge City Junior College, in Kansas.

When Larry arrived at the school, he found that he was not wanted. The old football coach had left, and the new one told him there was no automatic scholarship for him. He would have to earn it on the practice field. Lost and lonely in this hot, quiet town, Larry almost packed his bags for home. But he stayed on to prove he deserved the scholarship. It was almost a deadly mistake. One night he ran into some troublemakers in town. Someone shot at him, and the bullet tore through his hat, just missing his head.

Larry won his scholarship and worked hard for a losing team at Dodge City. After two seasons, the coach moved to Kansas State University. He was impressed with Larry and asked the young man to join him. At Kansas State, Larry found himself on yet another losing team. Even on a team that was lucky to win more than one game a year, Larry was so unknown that he started out on the bottom. It seemed that his life was going in circles, especially when he ran into another gunslinger. This time Larry dove to the floor to escape the shot.

Some of his rough childhood experiences suited Larry well as a hard-nosed blocker. Kansas State was so impressed with his blocking that Larry did

Larry Brown

not carry the ball as much as he would have liked. But blockers do not attract much attention. So when the pro scouts came around his senior year, Larry was again shuffled to the bottom of the pile. He was too small, too slow, and did not gain enough yards. The Washington Redskins waited until the eighth round of the 1969 draft before finally choosing him.

In Washington Larry finally joined a winning team. Washington's famous coach, Vince Lombardi, liked tough players who wanted to win, even if they were not the best. A fearless hitter such as Larry had a chance to catch the coach's eye, and so he began one last climb from the bottom. Larry was determined to prove he was as good as the famous college stars who were playing pro football.

Of course Larry had much to learn before he could be a star himself. His poor pass patterns drew ear-splitting screams from Lombardi. Larry also seemed to be late in starting each play. He refused to admit that he was deaf in his right ear and could not hear the signals. But the Redskins figured out the problem. They fitted his helmet with a hearing aid and placed him in the huddle with his good ear toward the quarterback. Still, Larry was nearly dropped from the squad because he had trouble catching passes in practice. But in exhibition games, his slippery fingers turned to glue, and he caught everything in sight.

Larry started the 1969 season on the bench. In Washington's first game, the regular runners moved like overloaded trucks. By halftime these players had only gained eight yards. An angry Lombardi

Larry used determination and his straight-ahead style of running to break away from opposing defenders.

sent Larry in for the second half. Immediately, Larry began picking up yards. He became the Redskins' best runner that year and ranked fourth in the league in yards gained.

Though he weighed only about 200 pounds, Larry carried the ball nearly 30 times a game for the next few years. Each time, he charged full speed into larger, stronger people. Because of this, he was often injured. He sometimes played in pain, but he never slowed down. Larry refused to fall to the ground without struggling for every inch he could get.

Larry's powerful legs earned him the NFL rushing title in 1970. In 1971 he gained 948 yards with only one healthy leg. Even so, few people took notice of him. He had been far from the spotlight all of his life, and it took time before his steady, hard running made sports headlines.

In 1972 Larry finally reached the top of the football world. That year he led Washington to the Super Bowl against Miami. During the game, Miami swarmed all over him, and he never had a chance to run. Washington lost the championship 14 to 7, but Larry's courage and determination impressed players and fans. He was chosen as the National Football Conference's Most Valuable Player for his efforts.

Several injuries in the next few years finally wore Larry down. By 1976 his football career was over. Even after all his success, few fans recognized his face. But the guy with the number 43 jersey worked his way to the top in pro football. When Larry remembers how long he had been on the bottom, he must be proud that the only thing he ever dodged were bullets.

9
Ron
LeFlore

No one could figure out why Ron LeFlore got into so much trouble when he was young. He did not come from a rough part of Detroit, and none of his sisters and brothers had problems with the police. But at the age of 11, Ron stole $1,000. When he got into safe-cracking, armed robbery, and parole-breaking, Ron found himself in deep trouble. In 1969, at only 17 years of age, he was sentenced to 5 to 15 years in prison.

Even in prison Ron got involved in fights. Because of his behavior, he was put in solitary confinement for more than three months at a time. Finally Ron found something in prison that changed his whole life: a baseball bat. Before this, he had never gone out for sports. But he was bored with prison life and joined the prison baseball team.

Ron LeFlore was first scouted by the Detroit Tigers while he was in prison.

Few people have ever learned the game as quickly as Ron did. Shortly before he was granted parole in 1973, he was averaging more than five hits for every 10 trips to the plate.

One day Ron received an unusual visitor—a Detroit Tigers' scout who wanted to see him play. Though the scout could see that Ron still needed to learn much about the game of baseball, he knew Ron had ability. When Ron was released from the prison a few weeks later, he joined one of the Tigers' minor league teams. Many players who have played baseball since they were children spend years in the minor leagues before they are ready for the major leagues. Yet Ron, a newcomer to the sport, found himself in the big leagues within a year.

Because of his inexperience, Ron made many errors at first. He dropped some fly balls and threw to the wrong base. But he worked hard and used his great speed to make up for those mistakes. Pitchers did not know what to expect from Ron. Sometimes they could make him swing at two bad pitches in a row, only to have him belt the third one for a hit.

Ron started his second full season with the Tigers as if he were going to break all hitting records. He kept Detroit fans on the edge of their seats by hitting in 30 straight games. This was the longest hitting streak in the American League in 27 years! His .316 batting average earned him a spot on the American League All-Star team. Even then, Ron got most of his hits by slapping the ball to right field.

In 1973 Ron learned to hit with power. Just when opponents had come to expect his soft pokes and line drives to right field, he socked 16 home runs and 10 triples. He also collected over 200 hits and crossed home plate exactly 100 times. Few players have ever achieved this in a single season.

But the most exciting part of Ron's game is not *how* he gets on base—it's what he does once he gets there. He may be the fastest man in baseball. In 1978 he led the American League with 68 stolen bases. His teammates found that it was easier to drive a run in with Ron on base. He could score from second base on practically any single that reached the outfield. His amazing total of 126 runs scored in 1978 also led the league. As he gained experience as a center fielder, he used his speed to cover a huge area of ground. Many experts predict that he will only get better in the years ahead.

70

Ron LeFlore

In 1979 Ron was traded to the Montreal Expos. He stole 97 bases for the Expos in 1980 to lead the entire National League. Fortunately for that league, Ron wasn't happy in Montreal, and in 1981 he signed as a free agent with the Chicago White Sox of the American League.

Like his ex-teammate, John Hiller, who survived a heart attack, Ron LeFlore found a new life in baseball. He also found that stealing does not pay— unless it's stealing bases!

In 1974 while pitching for Los Angeles, Tommy John's career appeared to be over when the tendon in his left elbow gave out.

10
Tommy
John

A major league baseball pitcher watches out for his pitching arm as if it were his life savings. His entire career depends on that one part of his body. Pitching is very hard on the arm. Countless numbers of pitchers have gone from strikeout kings to retired ballplayers because of an arm that suddenly went bad. It happened to Tommy John of the Los Angeles Dodgers one night in 1974. But remarkable courage and a medical breakthrough helped him return to become an even better pitcher than before.

Tommy was born in Indiana in 1943. As a child he received high marks in the classroom as well as on the playground. But what set him apart from other athletes was his remarkable pitch. At a very young age, he could throw a sinker ball. A sinker is a pitch that heads straight into the plate, only

73

to drop suddenly, just as the batter swings. Because of the way the ball sinks, a hitter usually pounds the ball into the dirt, giving the infielders a chance to throw him out.

Tommy started throwing his sinker for the Cleveland Indians' minor league teams in 1961. By his third season, he had worked his way up in the American League to the majors. He had not been there long before Cleveland traded him to the Chicago White Sox, where he developed into a reliable starting pitcher. In 1967 Tommy was enjoying his finest season when he was sidelined by an injury. After he recovered, he found little support from his weak-hitting White Sox teammates. Though he gave up just over three runs per game, Tommy was saddled with a losing record for three years in a row.

In 1972 Tommy found a fresh start in the National League. The White Sox traded him to the Los Angeles Dodgers. Following two good years of pitching, Tommy started out red-hot in 1974. By midseason he had won 13 games and lost only 3. Based on what happened in 1967, he might have suspected what was about to happen. Disaster had struck before when everything was going well.

Sure enough, on July 17, 1974, it happened. Tommy was pitching the same as he had for years when, without warning, his left elbow snapped. The tendon that held the elbow together had worn out just like an old shoelace. There was no way he could ever pitch again with his arm like that.

But Tommy was not willing to give up. He found an excellent surgeon, Dr. Frank Jobe, who performed two operations that had never been tried on a pitcher before. In the first operation, Dr. Jobe took a tendon from Tommy's right arm and put it in the elbow of Tommy's left arm. The second operation worked on the nerves of the left elbow. If this operation had failed, Tommy would have been left with an arm useless for pitching.

After recovering from these operations, Tommy found that he could toss the ball only about 30 feet. Still, he was determined to show up at the Dodgers' spring camp in 1975. When he got to the camp, his pitching looked pitiful. His hand could not grip the ball, and he could not even get his thumb wrapped around it. He could not make his pitches land even close to where he wanted them. But Tommy did not let this embarrass him. He taped his fingers to the ball to get them to

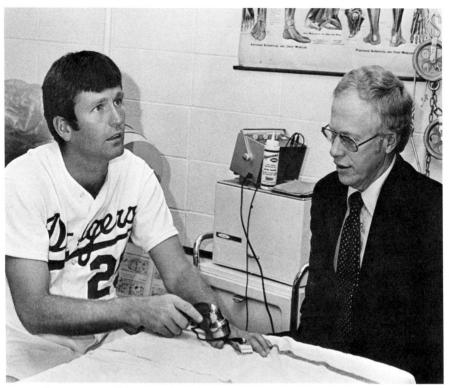

Two successful operations helped to put Tommy on the road to recovery.

grip correctly. Before every pitch, he used his right hand to force his thumb into place. He also made sure the rest of his body was in top shape while his left arm healed. He lifted weights and stepped up his running to as much as eight miles a day.

By July his arm nerves were healing. But it was not until February of 1976 that he regained full use of his pitching hand. He sharpened his control over his pitches and surprised the baseball world

76

After surgery, Tommy endured long hours of
therapy so that he could pitch again.

by winning 10 games the next season. For this
achievement, he was voted baseball's Comeback
Player of the Year. In 1977 he was pitching full
force. This time nothing spoiled his super season.
He won 20 games for the Dodgers, leading them to
the World Series.

In 1979 he signed with the New York Yankees
as a free agent. The smiling, friendly Tommy John
was a welcome relief to the quarrelsome Yankees.

Tommy made a remarkable comeback from his injury and has pitched better than ever since joining the New York Yankees in 1979.

78

Tommy continued serving up ground balls to his infielders and was named to the American League All-Star team.

Tommy considers himself just an average guy who kept himself in professional baseball through hard work and faith in God. But that doesn't mean he lacks confidence in himself. He talks almost nonstop when he is asked a question, especially about how long he plans to keep pitching. Though he has already lasted longer than most pitchers, he thinks he has several good seasons left in him. Tommy just may be a major league pitcher for a long time yet. After all, his arm is practically brand new.

ACKNOWLEDGMENTS: The photographs are reproduced through the courtesy of: pp. 4, 56, Los Angeles Rams; pp. 6, 76, 77, Los Angeles Dodgers, Mark Malone Photos; pp. 8, 13, 14, Philadelphia Flyers, Bernie Moser-Dufor Photographers; p. 11, Philadelphia Flyers; p. 19, Washington Bullets, Gary N. Fine Photo; pp. 21, 22, Washington Bullets; pp. 27, 29, 31, Pittsburgh Steelers; pp. 35, 36, 68, 71, Detroit Tigers; pp. 40, 44, Kitty O'Neil; p. 43, Kitty O'Neil, Stunts Unlimited; pp. 48, 50, Lee Trevino, Inc., Darst-Ireland Photography; p. 54, Buffalo Bills, Robert L. Smith Photography; p. 58, Philadelphia Eagles; pp. 60, 65, Washington Redskins, Paul Fine Photos-Nate Fine Productions; p. 63, Washington Redskins; p. 72, Los Angeles Dodgers; p. 78, New York Yankees.

Cover photograph: Vernon J. Biever

80